# Preface

Art therapy, including activities like coloring books, offers several benefits to adult clients with anxiety. It provides a creative and therapeutic outlet for individuals to express themselves and manage their anxiety in a non-verbal and non-threatening way.

Here are some of the benefits of art therapy, specifically through coloring books, for adults with anxiety:

- Stress Reduction, Mindfulness and Mindful Relaxation.
- Self-Expression, which is essential for expressing feelings, thoughts and emotions through colors selection and images.
- Distraction, which breaks the cycle of rumination;
- Improved Mood, with the releasing of natural mood lifters called endorphins.
- Sense of Accomplishment, that comes with the completion of a project.
- Emotional regulation, that colors bring to help regulate anxiety more effectively.
- Decreased Heart Rate and Blood Pressure, which is part of the physiological benefits of color expression.
- Self-Awareness for the client as well as helpful insight for the therapist, through colors selection.
- Social Connection. This is a great way to participate in a group therapy experience.
- Coping Skills. Art therapy can help individuals develop and practice coping skills that they can apply in their daily lives when faced with anxiety-provoking situations.

Anthony T. Hines  LCMHC

# Coloring Tips and More to Explore!

Dear Colorist,

To ensure the best coloring experience and preserve the beauty of each page in your 'Serene Things Art Therapy Coloring' book, we recommend using color pencils. Unlike markers or paints, color pencils provide precise control and vibrant results without the risk of bleeding onto the next page.

Color Pencils:
- Choose a variety of colors to bring your artwork to life.
- Layer colors for depth and shading.
- Experiment with different techniques like hatching and blending.
- Shading has been included on some images to add dimension to your coloring experience. Try using coordinating colors for the shaded areas to make your final work pop.

In future volumes, we'll delve in and discover new horizons of serenity and tranquility.

Happy Coloring!

# Serene Things
# Art Therapy Coloring

## Volume 1: Finding Serenity

"As you embark on this coloring journey, remember that the world is full of wonders, and serenity eagerly awaits those who seek it. Embrace the beauty of each stroke, for within your creativity, you'll find tranquility and joy."

"Behold the tranquil ballet of dandelions as they disperse their seedlings, dancing gracefully on the gentle breath of the wind."

"Take in the aroma of nature's essences as you bicycle down a country road."

"Some find the serenity of fishing at the lake, a peaceful retreat."

"Playful otters near a riverbanks clear peaceful waters, observe a new day."

"In the quiet stillness, senerity can be found in the peaceful serenade of frogs taking in the morning air."

"Enjoy natures serenade , while taking a peaceful boat ride on a tranquil lake ."

"Amidst the gentle babble of the brook, find your tranquil haven."

"Behold the vibrant spirit of the peacock as its majestic feathers unfold in a symphony of colors."

"Swaying in serenity, where time and worries fade away."

" Celebrate serenity with each barefoot journey, as tiny grains of sand hug your toes"

"Chickadee birds perched on snowy branches in a calm winter forest."

"A butterfly dances around the ephemeral beauty of the dandelion"

"In the silence of meditation, the soul finds serenity."

"Tranquility blooms in the Zen garden's silent beauty."

" Koi fish are often depicted in pairs, symbolizing the concept of yin and yang and the balance of nature."

"There is beauty and serenity as small purple crocuses break forth from the snow covered ground"

"Turtle's basking in the sun, enjoying nature's bounty."

"Adorable owls perch quietly in a tree, in a peaceful woodland retreat."

" Observing nature as a turtle watches over it's hachlings in their sandy beach cradle."

"On horseback, a peaceful excursion in the lush, green expanse, brings a calming escape."

"With music in my ears and a cozy chair beneath, I find serenity."

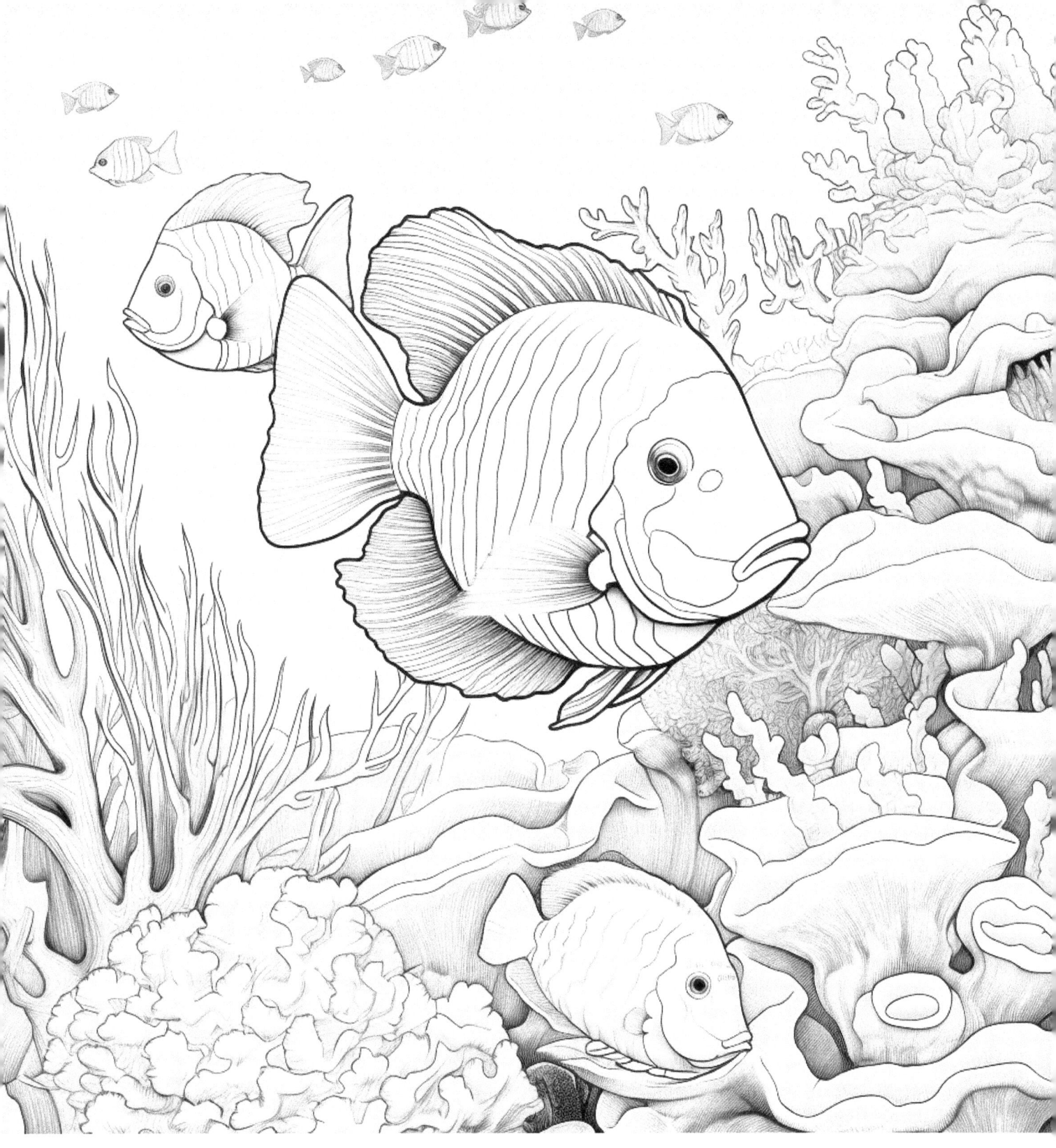

"Vibrant tropical fish swimming in harmony among intricate coral formations."

"A quiet bamboo grove, unveils a panda peacefully munching on bamboo shoots."

"Amidst the lily pads, serenity finds its voice, Ribit, Ribit."

"Graceful swans gliding on the calm surface of a pristine, mirror-like lake."

"I love the sound of the asphalt against the tires, as I take in the beautiful landscape."

"Elegant gazelles grazing peacefully on the African savannah."

"Peaceful dreams in the cradle of innocence."

"Graceful flamingos wading in the still waters of a peaceful lagoon."

"As the cozy fireplace flames dance, let the story within your book ignite your imagination."

"Amidst the gentle hum of bees and the vibrant blooms, find the tranquil serenity of nature's pollination dance."

"Listening to the rhythmic melody of a tranquil waterfall cascade, brings a sense of peace and wonder."

"As dragonflies dance on still waters, so does serenity dance within our souls."

"Embrace the serenity of majestic waters, where lush, tree-lined shores await your creative touch."

"In the heart of the mountains, find solace with every step of your breathtaking journey."

"Waking to the cheerful song of birds in a cherry blossom tree."

"Under the moon's gentle glow, a pair of owls fills the night with their melodious 'Whooo Whooo.'"

"Amid the crackling of the campfire, nature's enigmatic melodies join the night's serenade."

"Embrace the beauty of each stroke, for within your creativity, you'll find tranquility and joy."

Thank you for joining me in this exploration of serenity. There is so much more to discover, within ourselves and the world around us. Embrace tranquility, for it is a gateway to countless discoveries and boundless beauty.

Don't forget to explore our website for more coloring books, coloring pages, and creative inspiration. Scan the QR code located at the back cover of this book, or visit *www.serene-things.com* to discover a world of coloring possibilities.

*Cynthia Lisette Mozingo*

www.ingramcontent.com/pod-product-compliance
Lightning Source LLC
Chambersburg PA
CBHW081507040426
42446CB00017B/3429